Wings & Vengeance - A Journey through Poems

Tarun Kumar Bandarupally

BookLeaf
Publishing

India | USA | UK

Presentation by *BookLeaf Publishing*

Web: www.bookleafpub.com

E-mail: info@bookleafpub.com

ISBN: 9789357446433

First edition 2022

DEDICATION

This book is dedicated to Rajinikanth, because why not?

ACKNOWLEDGEMENT

Well! Well! Well! Writing this book was quite challenging but turned out to be even more rewarding to my evolution as a person. None of this would have been possible without my birth. So, thanks to my parents and their parents. Special thanks to all my well-wishers and haters (Hope you are not). I stumbled upon this 21 day – 21 poems challenge by BookLeaf Publishers and I'm whole-heartedly grateful to the universe for letting this happen.

PREFACE

Ever considered the idea of journalizing your thoughts regularly and revisiting them at the end of 21 days? This is precisely the kind of ride you will be experiencing through the pages. With every passing second, our neurons keep firing and get bombarded with a variety of thoughts influenced by our immediate surroundings and concealed memories. Add a vivid sense of imagination to it, you will observe that there is a harmony when the same is penned down. A poem in its own sense articulates my soul. In fact, life in itself is a poem in a way. These compilations expose my deep-rooted love for nature, my observations on relationships, and a metaphorical approach on how we all are in tune with the universe. Enjoy the journey...

Man with a can

It's the tenth of September and 10 PM now,
I'm attempting a poem, no idea how.
Thoughts become things is what I've learnt,
My room has things, but its thoughts seem burnt.

Trees outside are swaying along the breeze,
Did that rhyme? I'm having a good time.
My window's half open, so is my world,
Verbs for rattling flora? Maybe 'twirled'.

A flamboyant fly is fluttering its floppy wings,
Eyeing my bowl, but the window mesh stings.
Meanwhile, crickets are chirping about life in monotone,
Tried Onomatopoeia and alliteration, but a lot more to hone.

A cloaked bloke with a fluorescent pail just zoomed past,
To make it dramatic, I'll call him a sorcerer.
The clock's ticking; it's time for supper,
Until then, watch out for a man with a can.

What am I?

What have I become?
Something I've never imagined.

What am I writing?
Something I've never witnessed.

What am I picturing?
Something I've never seen.

What am I asking?
Something I've never received.

What am I conveying?
Something I've just thought of.

Covid - A Haiku

Stifling vaccine noon-
A quick corona cackle
whilst watching their death

Ode to the Damsel

My enchantress, you inspire me to write.
I adore the way you amble, smile, and dance,
Invading my mind day and through the night,
Always dream about our flowering romance.

Your eyelashes remind me of a radiant quill,
Emanate grace, elegance, and poise.
Extra glint and sparkle in the month of April,
Peace blooms with your aura and showers me
with joys.

How do I love you? Let me count the ways.
Your flowing hair, glowing mind, and charming
eyes.
The thought of your glittering presence fills my
days.
My love for you is a tearful surprise.

Now I must depart with a heavy heart,
Recall my fervent words whilst we're apart.

Venus Fly Cat-Limerick

Once there was a cat from outer space,
That trimmed its whiskers and covered its face.
On each stormy day,
She would say,
'Oh! How I miss my race!

The Legend of Her

A mercurial tale of an enigma,
Termed as stigma by the society,
Dejected, depressed and down at eighteen,
The smile never betrayed her childhood trauma.

Come the twenties, renamed Bipolar,
The therapist was warm but friends, brick walls.
Highs were euphoric and lows were suicidal,
Medications bridged the gap but tethered to the
trap.

Her heart, thoughts and mind caused mayhem,
Onlookers chirped, "Calm down, else you'll
implode!"
Self-harm and Lithium supplanted her regime,
As hallucinations decided: physical subsides
emotional pain.

She accepted her condition, ignited her
redemption,
Welcomed meditation and examined her
medication.
With neither a clear destination nor a lack of
dedication,
She picked herself up and expanded beyond the
material world.

The 'Switch'

The tiny switch glowed, and so did his life.

The circuit appeared flawed, so he gripped his knife.

Just like the moon, he had a dark side.

Little did he know that he was being spied.

He sprinted out fuming, butchered everything in his way.

The agent picked up his pen and went on with his day.

'Pet'ty

He was born blind,
She was born with a gift.

He could sometimes see people in the dark,
She could hear the thoughts of animals.

His mind painted intricate pictures,
Her gift made her an excellent veterinarian.

He saw his grandfather for a whole day last year,
She had a visitor (client) with a patient.

His grandfather expired that night,
The client wanted her pet to be put down.

He could then see everyone in his family, but the
person his sister was talking to,
She heard the pet scream, "Spare me, and your
family will be safe".

She set the pet free and he could only see the
client of hers.

Leafy Haiku

The floating maple-
Raining dry foliage, click!
But, it's spring! What? How?

It seems

It seems like the sky is melting,
It seems like the heart of the clouds is opening
up,
It seems like the raindrop on his forehead is
revitalizing,
It seems like the most alive moment he has ever
witnessed,
It seems like he is inebriated.

Farewell Winter

The spring sun rises
With an aesthetic vibe,
Keen to permeate.

The mornings wrap her like a warm blanket
With rays kissing her forehead,
And rejuvenating her.

Her senses elevate to
The aroma of pristine lilacs
And breeze choreographed lavenders
In her backyard.

The sparkling butterflies wander
In pursuit of
Sweet elixir from flora.

The Golden Star begs for her attention,
She lifts her delicate chin,
With eyes fully closed,
And smiles to the heavens.

Bioluminescent Realization

Starlit waves
And twinkling Sea Sparkles
Swerve in melody
Intricately orchestrated by
The glorious full moon.

Tiny droplets
Tap against
Her conical enclosure.
Some leave a mark,
Some trickle down in a pattern.

She is rejoicing this sight
With her cheeks
Cradled in her palms
And mouth wide open.

A thought lingers;
What's live (spelt) backwards?
It is evil...to live in reverse
"Stay in the moment", she realizes

And, the enlightened soul never looked back
since.

Love – A Healing Force

Beyond his beaming masquerade, what was concealed?
A hot-tempered brain with lack of empathy,
A grandiose soul with glaring apathy.
Sharp tunnel vision and drive to succeed,
Mercurial self-esteem with validation in need.

He did have a soul but was dark and twisted,
The relationship was toxic but somehow persisted.
Kudos to her patience despite no reciprocation,
She was needy so lowered her expectation.
Was he a psychopath or a sadist?
She, being a therapist, marked him as a narcissist.
His loneliness was quite evident
And narc reflexes fairly prominent.

He listened to her for once and looked inward,
The emptiness was craving to be altered.
With time, he understood that no one's below or above,

And there's nothing in this world that cannot be healed through love.

Wings and Vengeance

Like a butterfly
That lost her ability to fly,
He zoned out from reality.
Every decision entailed agony,
Every organ bled profusely,
Every thought extinguished creativity,
Every utterance led to misery,
Every breath rekindled morosity,
Every blink distanced him from redemption,
And vengeance flowered within.

You

Your lips may lie but your eyes can't,
The glint is evident as your brows slant.
You take a step, I'll take a leap,
Let's confess already as we know it's deep.

What got us here won't get us there,
If we live under our shadows, stand and stare.
Every passing second takes us closer to our
grave,
So, I want you; I need you as you are the feeling
I always crave.

Happily Married?

To visit her parents she needs permission and
explanations,
These hurdles alienate her impressions.

To step out, she is tagged along with a known
person,
This is one of the several modes of coercion.

At every age, she is to be accompanied by a
familiar face,
When it comes to marriage, it's a bribe
demanding stranger from a foreign place.

The seventh step exposes the gap between
herself and her own,
She swallows the emotion and becomes the
opposite of her clone.

She loses her right to dream,
Bearing kids and raising them is her new regime.

Marriage changes her home, city, and her
surname but not her tender mind,
Stays tethered to the warm conversations and
memories with her kind.

Life as we see it

Once upon a time,
On a pleasant cloudy dawn,
An army of caterpillars,
Was dancing through,
Its cycle of life.

Her innocent eyes
Captured that delight
And she returned
At a spectacular moment.

The silent army
Opened its wings
One after the other
And flew across the open field.

The Butterflies danced around
For a few fortnights
And disappeared.
It's a cloudy dawn today,
And there's a new army.

Do you even know him? - A Tanka

His alter ego
Is pretty dark and cryptic.
It takes many forms
And exotic dimensions
When it sneers, he feels frightened.

What is Nature?

Dance to the tune of our nature,
Without inhibitions, without any strings,
Like a ray of light piercing the dawn mist,
Like the moon shining amidst dark clouds,
Like a moth in pursuit of light,
Like a brook babbling in monsoon,
Like a baby sloth falling asleep.

Close your eyes
To discover your nature.
Soothing darkness
Stills your pulse.
Your nimble feet
Need no ground to dance
And the stage feels infinite.

Here's my story

I stand alone in the middle of a broken road
I'm trapped inside a well of uncertainty
Every moment, I stare at the cosmos,
Unbiased towards day and night.
The blazing sun shrinks my life sip by sip.
Whirring tyres ruffle my meditation,
But I find peace in quenching the thirst of birds.

I was in a river but somehow ended up here,
Trying to build a theory but the darkness is eerie.
I'm now friends with the mud.
Brings his buddies and enjoys my shelter.
We share experiences and are growing stronger.
I sense I'm about to pass in a moment,
Ahh! The hot tar hurts but I feel liberated.

Goodbye everyone! By the way, I'm a Water
Puddle.

Birdman

Just like birds fly away from home during
winter,
He keeps running in the direction of the sun.

They travel in pursuit of warmth,
He travels to avoid the dark.

Their nests are empty,
His heart is void.

They close their eyes for rest and solace,
His eyes are forced shut, worn out and darkness
prevails.